My Beloved Daughter

Jean Parthat

Copyright © 2018 Jean Parthat.

All rights reserved. No part of this book may be used or reproduced by any means, graphic, electronic, or mechanical, including photocopying, recording, taping or by any information storage retrieval system without the written permission of the author except in the case of brief quotations embodied in critical articles and reviews.

This book is a work of non-fiction. Unless otherwise noted, the author and the publisher make no explicit guarantees as to the accuracy of the information contained in this book and in some cases, names of people and places have been altered to protect their privacy.

NIV: Scriptures taken from the Holy Bible, New International Version®, NIV®. Copyright © 1973, 1978, 1984, 2011 by Biblica, Inc.™ Used by permission of Zondervan. All rights reserved worldwide. www.zondervan.com The "NIV" and "New International Version" are trademarks registered in the United States Patent and Trademark Office by Biblica, Inc.
LifeRich Publishing is a registered trademark of
The Reader's Digest Association, Inc.

LifeRich Publishing books may be ordered through booksellers or by contacting:

LifeRich Publishing
1663 Liberty Drive
Bloomington, IN 47403
www.liferichpublishing.com
1 (888) 238-8637

Because of the dynamic nature of the Internet, any web addresses or links contained in this book may have changed since publication and may no longer be valid. The views expressed in this work are solely those of the author and do not necessarily reflect the views of the publisher, and the publisher hereby disclaims any responsibility for them.

Any people depicted in stock imagery provided by Thinkstock are models, and such images are being used for illustrative purposes only.
Certain stock imagery © Thinkstock.

ISBN: 978-1-4897-1544-9 (sc)
ISBN: 978-1-4897-1545-6 (hc)
ISBN: 978-1-4897-1546-3 (e)

Library of Congress Control Number: 2018901077

Print information available on the last page.

LifeRich Publishing rev. date: 02/08/2018

Preface — My Beloved Daughter

This book is written at the Lord Jesus Christ's leading. I believe this book to be written in accordance with His will. I have tried to make every detail accurate, but even after a few days or in my case, a few hours, some things do not set as clear a picture in my mind as they should. It is actually now twenty some years later and I have decided, with the Lord's prompting, it is now or never; I must complete this book.

The writing actually began on Day 4, Friday, but I was led to the desire to write this halfway through Day 1. I have mentally gone back to relive this experience as it happened because the emotions and the obedience to the Lord Jesus Christ can only be captured in reliving it. I realize as I finish the last chapter that this story is not over, but forever continuing. This is not a storybook tale; this is the story of the life of a teenager and how that life intertwines with her mother and another friend.

This is the story of the Power of Faith and the Power of Prayer. This is the story of God's work being done in three ordinary, everyday people. This is the story of God's faithfulness to those who seek Him.

Contents

Preface — My Beloved Daughter v

Chapter 1   In The Beginning: The Early Years 1
Chapter 2   Finding Out 11
Chapter 3   Trip Day: New York, Here I Come! 21
Chapter 4   NYC Day 1 : Looking For ∀ 29
Chapter 5   NYC Day 2: Looking 39
Chapter 6   NYC Day 2: Found 51
Chapter 7   Day 3: Flight To Houston 69
Chapter 8   ∀'s Path to Addiction 79
Chapter 9   Houston – the Days After 85
Chapter 10 The Years After 101
About the Author 107

ONE

In The Beginning: The Early Years

When I think about the day my daughter was born, I remember an awesome feeling of newness, the anticipation of beginning a journey. Our first child was greatly desired and arrived two weeks early, much to our pleasant surprise. My husband and I had been married for a little over two years and now looking forward to a family. Baby∀ was so tiny, so dependent, and I wondered how things would go in her life. What would Baby∀ grow up to be? I was determined that my daughter would not be pampered nor would she be spoiled. My husband and I would raise Baby∀ just right!

Baby∀'s young life started off very well. She grew quickly, her progress being noted in the usual baby book. She was doing all the right things at all the right times, except for growing her teeth. Baby∀ didn't seem to be able to grow teeth; at least no teeth seemed to be able to break through her gums. She never had her first tooth until she was twenty-one and one-half months old! But she sure could gum corn-on-the-cob or steak when these foods were presented to her.

When Baby∀ was fourteen and one-half months old, her brother was born. He was a healthy baby and like Baby ∀ started sleeping through the night at one month old. Because Baby∀ and her brother were so close in age, they grew up much like twins. After Baby ∀'s brother turned two years old, both children were doing pretty much the same things at the same time as far as motor skills went.

Girl∀ began school at four and one-half at a neighborhood school. Before she began school, Girl∀ was very advanced and continued to forge ahead in school, reading quickly and finding her niche in the young academic field.

When Girl∀ was in fifth grade she tried out and was chosen for the part of Nana in the children's play, The Velveteen Rabbit. Girl∀ had always been an "actress" and she really blossomed in the theatrical world in this musical production. From here on in, her theater career was launched. She had also been taking piano lessons since she was four years old and had developed quite a bit of musical talent.

As Girl∀ continued to grow and develop, her father and I encouraged her individuality. We both promoted our children's independence, all the while instructing them in knowledge of the world. As Girl∀ grew she became more and more content being by herself. She could always entertain herself with a myriad of projects and activities. I knew she preferred to be alone and I didn't concern myself with this facet of her personality because I enjoy lone times also.

When Teen∀ entered eighth grade she was beginning to feel different and making friends with people who I thought were quite different from whom I perceived her to be. Teen∀ always had a heart for people who were outcasts such as the homeless, drug users, and homosexuals. However, now she was beginning to join these groups in their thoughts and ideas. Was it to try to understand so she would know how to help them? Or was she becoming involved so she could be one of them? I just didn't know.

In February of Teen∀'s ninth grade school year, her father left one Friday night. He packed up his clothes in his truck and he left his family. I guess I can tell you what a crisis this put the remaining family in. For anyone who has experienced this trauma, you know what I'm writing about; for anyone who has not been in this situation, let me share that it is devastating not only to the mate left behind, but especially to the children. He moved at first to his mother's house, a five-minute ride across town. Within a few weeks he had moved into an apartment with a former girlfriend. Life sure was difficult during that time, especially for Teen∀. It seemed that Teen∀'s father rejected her. Things were ok between Teen∀'s brother and her father, but dad could not seem to deal with Teen ∀. About a week before he moved out of our house, Teen ∀ had told her dad she was having homosexual feelings. I understood it to be a normal experience for Teen∀'s age of fourteen, but her father did not understand that. Things then became much worse for Teen∀ than they had been. It reached a point that Teen∀ began to feel so badly about herself that she started looking for ways of escaping.

About one and one-half months later Teen∀ went to a dance. She had a very bad experience there and when she came home she went to bed. So did I until 3am when Teen ∀ woke me up and said she did something stupid. She said she took a few aspirin. I asked her how many and she said five or six. I asked her how she felt and she said tired. I decided to lay down with her on her bed to keep an eye on her. She seemed ok. I checked her a few times during the night and as Sunday morning arrived, I prepared for church. Teen∀, her brother and I all sang in the church choir so we went early to church. When it came time to go into the sanctuary, Teen∀ said she didn't feel well enough so I told her to sit in the choir room and we'd touch base after the service. By then, I had decided to take Teen∀ to the hospital if she were not better in one-half hour. She wasn't better so we went to the local hospital. There I learned that her 'five or six' aspirin were many more. It had however been much too long a time to pump her stomach so Teen∀ was admitted for observation. By the end of the day Teen∀ couldn't assure her doctor that she wouldn't try suicide again, so she was then moved to the Mental Health Unit. Teen∀ was not happy with this move and it was so hard for me to drive away from the hospital that day. My daughter is only fourteen and one-half. How could this be happening to her? Her stay was short and once she arrived back home, I thought she was doing well until about a month later when she asked me to take her back to the Mental Health Unit because she was afraid she would hurt herself again.

After these experiences Teen∀ went through three more very difficult years of continuing to grow up, years of learning who she was, or at least who she thought she was, years of thinking about her future, and years of depression, rejection, anger and rebellion.

Then my daughter made a decision that she wanted to go to the Fashion Institute of Technology in New York City to study art. She was pretty much an A student and we both thought she would be accepted into their fine arts program, even though it was very selective. She was accepted and began her first year at FIT. Teen∀ did ok. When she went back to the city for her second year she then lived in an apartment with another person she did not know. Her schoolwork was now going downhill and she started withdrawing from life. At this point in the late fall, Teen∀ decided to drop out of school so she wouldn't fail out at the end of the semester. But, she was determined to remain in New York City. My daughter was now eighteen and I could not change her mind. During the winter and spring we kept in touch with a telephone call on occasion. I thought things were fine for my daughter. Little did I know the real truth about Teen∀'s life.

TWO
Finding Out

I tried to call ∀ at her boyfriend's house on Long Island, as this is where she was staying until she got an apartment. I left a message for her to call me when she got home. She would call within a day or two as was the case in the past when I was unable to reach her and left a message. I waited one week, but no phone call. I thought maybe she had not received the message from whom I spoke with one week ago so I called again. This time I reached her boyfriend's mom and spoke with her. As the conversation progressed, Susan felt she needed to let me know where ∀ was working. She explained the type of job as a worker in a "girly" show. I was shocked, as my daughter had told me she was a telemarketer. Susan went on to explain she had asked ∀ to leave her house that very day; she had overstayed her welcome. After ∀ had moved out of her apartment at FIT, she had been staying at her boyfriend's house. She had been there for one month with the intention of staying only two weeks. I asked Susan if she knew where ∀ was moving to and she said she thought ∀ had moved to another apartment. Immediately I sensed a nudge in my spirit; something was not right with ∀! I felt a real blackness in my spirit about ∀ and sensed she was in trouble. Then Susan went on to say that ∀ had indicated I would be down to pick up her things stored at the house. My fear was confirmed; things were not right. ∀ had never called to ask me to pick up her things. What could I do to help my daughter? What did God want me to do to help her? How was I to get ∀'s things back from New York City when I was working so many hours seven days a week? I needed to pray about this.

I thought of my friend Mel who had just recently come back into my life after an absence of thirteen years. I had lived next door to Mel, her husband and two children and we became fast friends, our children playing together, Mel and I grocery shopping together on Wednesdays, going downtown together with our strollers, sewing together, even eating together at the counter of the Grants store with our children. But when ∀ was five, Mel moved and then after a short time she and her husband divorced and Mel moved to Texas. We no longer kept up with each other and I didn't see her for about thirteen years until just recently at my church. She had come to church with her son who was now going with one of the girls in my son's youth group. When Mel moved to Texas her sons had remained in town with her ex-husband. What a surprise it was to see Mel after all that time had passed. Neither of us knew Jesus Christ when we parted so many years before, but now we both knew the Lord as our savior. As we talked, Mel told me she had settled into a home with a family she knew on Long Island. She was working for a firm there and was doing fine. Her son was graduating in a couple of weeks from the local high school near me. Mel would be coming for his graduation.

Midweek I decided to call Mel and see if she could pick up ∀'s things when she came up for her son's graduation. After all, I discovered she lived about ten minutes from Susan's house. Mel was willing to pick up ∀'s things and help me out of a bind. Mel said she would possibly arrive around 10:00pm Friday night. At 9:30pm Mel was at the house. Her car was loaded, the trunk, the seats, the floors, all totally full. Mel and I started unloading the trunk of the car and I decided to call my son to help with the amplifier and heavier things. Mel looked at me and said, "You should see her scrapbooks. She's really messed up." Mel, my son and I started looking for clues as to where ∀ might be in NYC. What I discovered as I looked at these pieces of my daughter's life was a very hurt, destructive girl. I knew things had been difficult for ∀ in New York

City, but I was not prepared for the destructive life she was leading. Her scrapbooks and letters indicated that she was doing drugs daily (although I did not know what kind), she was working as a stripper at a business on 42nd and 8th called Showworld, and she was homeless, maybe living in an abandoned building on 11th and Area B&C. I was not angry with her. God was sure building up my motherly feelings of love. As a matter of fact, I believe now that I loved my daughter with the love Jesus had for her (1John 3:1). I've always loved my daughter a great deal, but God gave me unconditional love for her. We can only love unconditionally as God loves when He helps us. Without His love, I surely would have been saying, "What a mess, ∀. You really did it now. How could you have messed your life up so badly?" But I didn't feel that way at all. God gave me such a protective instinct toward ∀ that I just wanted to help her and protect her. There was absolutely no condemnation. How I hurt for my daughter. What could I do? I knew in an instant I would have to go to New York City and get my precious daughter out of there. That very night we prayed for ∀ and our mission. Chills came over me as I prayed and asked God to protect my child and soften her heart for my arrival in New York City. I knew God was listening to my every word and hearing my mother's heart cry out for my child, His child. I believe from that moment God gave me His eyes and His heart for His precious child, my daughter. My only desire was to get her out of New York City. There was work to be done! But where was I to start? Things started to become clear in my mind now.

I now had to make a decision about what to do with ∀'s things. I put some things like her "trip" journal and other negative writings and drawings in a bag to be carefully tucked away until such time as I felt I could safely give these back to ∀. I put the bag in with my personal effects at the bank where I worked and kept it there for two years, when I felt a time had come that ∀ could deal with all this heinous material. I asked friends at my church if they would store a big bag of things I deemed inappropriate for ∀ at this time. The next month I did retrieve ∀'s things from them. Now it was wait until the Lord gave me direction.

My son had asked to go to New York City on Sunday to do some 'scouting around' to see if he could determine where ∀ was. I had taken money out of the bank for him to take, but as Sunday approached, he said that he did not feel God was leading him to go (John 10;27). This was not the right timing; I had to wait! But how long? After all, ∀ could die any day from an overdose of the drugs she was taking. If she was homeless as we suspected, she could fall into any number of grave situations. How long was I to wait?

My answer came that very Sunday. After church I was home reading from a spiritual warfare manual, Strongman's His Name, What's His Game? I got well into binding evil spirits and casting them away from ∀. I was heavily into prayer and even tired to the point of drifting off when I jerked with a start. I had the sensation in my hand of crushing a glass ball and then a warmth just seemed to pervade my being. I immediately felt that Satan's hold on my daughter had been crushed just as I had figuratively crushed that glass ball in my hand. July 4th was less than two weeks away, but that is when I would find her. God had given me a sure knowledge of that. I needed two days to go to New York City. I would leave the following Monday. The power of prayers, mine and everyone else's praying for us, had given rise to a miracle. This was a turning point in my own faith. This was when I really began to learn about the power of prayer and the power of trusting in God – FAITH.

The confirmation of this vision was not long in coming. The very next Sunday in church, one of my

Thursday night prayer group friends approached me to share what God had laid on her heart. She told me that as the Thursday night group was praying for ∀, she felt the Holy Spirit had been working in ∀ that week. That was the confirmation I needed to hear. Satan's power in ∀ was shattered and God's power was dominating again. What a victory! I was to need many more victories and I was to receive many more victories!

THREE
Trip Day: New York, Here I Come!

I awoke early Monday morning with the thought to hurry up and get my preparations for the trip completed before I go to work. My intention was to head to Mel's house on Long island as soon as I finished work, around 5:30pm. Mel was to meet me at the Thruway's Ramapo rest stop, the stop closest to the Tappan Zee Bridge. From there, Mel would take me on a shortcut to New Hyde Park where she lived. Then we would awake refreshed the next day for our trip into New York City. Mel had agreed to go with me to New York City to help find ∀. She had taken vacation days so she could help me. She knew a lot more about New York City than I did. I had only been there about four or five times before. I did not doubt for a minute that we would find ∀ as the Lord had encouraged. I also knew that Mel's help would be invaluable. She knew the city. I was amazed how God provided a long ago friend, sending her back into my life at just the right time to help me find my wayward daughter.

I still had to pack, but even before that I had to wash the clothes I intended to take with me. I had purchased clothes for ∀, suspecting that she had very little to her name at this point and I needed to wash these clothes also. I had to buy oil and automatic transmission fluid for my car. I also needed to purchase gasoline, dog food, and shampoo for home, as I had no idea how long I would be away. I quickly showered, ironed some clothes to wear to work and packed my bags. One bag had my Bible and books that I was working from plus the books from ∀'s things that I felt would be important to take to the hospital, where I had intended to bring her to when we found her. These I had wrapped in plastic. ∀ need not know I had these with me.

Finally, after accomplishing everything needing to be done, I flew out of the house. It was a relief to get to work and start my job. I was so tied up with preparations for New York City that my free time was nonexistent. I kept thinking I had to cash my husband's check he had given to help with expenses. Should I get some traveler's checks or should I carry the money? I really didn't want to carry a lot of money with me. After all, I had no idea where in New York City I would find myself looking for ∀. I didn't even know what possible predicament I could find myself in. Only the Lord knew that for sure. I knew that I would find ∀, but I had no assurance she would go voluntarily with me and this she had to do to sign herself into a hospital. ∀ was now 19 years old and no longer a minor. What would I do if she said no? Would I stay in New York City and just plead and wait? What if the people she worked for would not let her go? I had no idea what kind of escapade I was in for. After calling two airlines I discovered that travelers checks could be used to pay for my airfare so I decided to convert $650 of my husband's check into travelers checks and the other $350 I put into my account knowing full well I could use my ATM card to access money when I needed it. I still had the $100 that I had withdrawn from my account the week before when my son had planned to go to New York City to search for his sister. That would be plenty of cash to take with me, a little hidden in each sock and some in my pants pockets.

As the day progressed I seemed to relax much more. I knew this whole ordeal was in God's hands and I wasn't about to change anything. I called Rapha and left a message to speak with Marge who I had been in contact with after I discovered my daughter's need. I was beginning to feel a little bit uncertain about Rapha's help. I trusted Marge whom I had spoken to, but I thought how can they make all this happen? I needed to confirm that when I found ∀, Rapha could indeed get her on a plane to the hospital. And where that hospital would be located, no one knew. I would call back a little later. I was beginning to look forward to closing time and balancing both my teller box and the office at the bank I worked at. I had hoped to be out by 5:30pm. I hoped my boss would let me leave after I balanced my teller box; after all, I stayed every day to balance the office afterwards. There were other tellers. When we closed the bank I got to work right away and balanced my teller box. I was off by a penny. I liked being exact, but after all, I had opened a wrap of pennies today and not counted them before I started using them. I quickly ran my totals, put my money in the vault and asked my boss if I could go. Sure thing. Great, it was only 5:30pm. I had to recall Rapha to speak with Marge about my daughter's insurance. I was put on the line with a gentleman who asked how he could help me. I explained my circumstances to him asking where Marge was. I had just missed her again. I explained to this gentleman that I was on my way to New York City in a few minutes and I wanted to be sure that I could get my daughter into a hospital when I found her. Marge was to let me know about ∀'s insurance coverage. I also told him I was really uneasy about going to New York City to get my daughter if this had not yet been set up. He let me know he understood how I felt and went about the business of checking my daughter's insurance. He said everything was fine with her insurance and why didn't I call Marge tomorrow. As I was hanging up the phone, the head teller approached me waving something in her hand. It was a vault ticket which meant that I had received money from either the vault or another teller. She told me she found this under my terminal and it didn't look like it had been processed. I looked at it and agreed that it had not been processed, which meant I had a big problem. Well, how did I balance my teller box? We started looking at where I could have made a mistake. I had made three errors that day which, when combined, fit together in such a way so as to appear that I had balanced. God had already given me the knowledge that this would be a humorous experience. "It's starting", I said. "The Lord's humor is starting". I was glad I had not left the building yet, leaving all my errors to the rest of our group. My boss said she would redo my totals and I could be on my way. Now I finally was headed to New York City.

FOUR
NYC Day 1: Looking For ∀

Early! We were up really early. I was awake with a pounding headache. It was 5:00am or earlier. I never watch a clock, but I can usually guess fairly close to the exact time. I lay in bed for about one-half hour and then I decided I'd better sit up. I must get rid of this headache. Mel awoke and asked about coffee or tea. I'm not a coffee drinker, but tea sure sounded good. I could still fast, but just drink the tea. I had felt the leading from the Lord to fast (Matt 6:17,18) beginning yesterday morning. I was not the least bit hungry. When you fast at the Lord's calling, you never seem to get hungry.

As I sat down at the table to drink my tea, the man who owned the house came over and sat down. He was awakened by the smell of the coffee Mel had started perking so she could begin her day. Sandy asked a few questions which I good-naturedly answered. Then he asked if ∀ was really a born-again Christian. "Yes, I believe she is", I said with some doubt. Sandy asked me to pray about that. I went into Mel's room to get my Bible; I needed scripture right then. We got back to the table and Sandy had some more observations and suggestions. He then took the time to pray about my situation. As we prayed I felt led to ask that God's will be done in the whole situation (Luke 22:42). I really didn't have a clue as to when within the next two days ∀ would be found or in what condition. The only thing I knew for certain was that I would find her by the end of tomorrow. Sandy had a problem with my prayer. "If you don't know what the Lord's will is, you'd better pray about it." I told Sandy that I did know the Lord's will was for me to find ∀ in the next two days, but I had no idea how He would execute this feat. After all, New York City was a pretty big place to look for someone when you really didn't know where she was located in the city! Sandy continued to pump God's Word into my ears and my mind. It was reassuring to hear the familiar passages of scripture.

Finally, it was time for me to shower and prepare to go into the city. Let's see, twenty dollars in this sock, twenty dollars in the other sock. I had no idea what I would encounter. I figured if I was going to get beat up, the person accosting me would not get everything I had.

Mel and I headed into the city. It was a beautiful July day. Where would we start? "Where exactly did ∀ say the abandoned building was", I asked Mel? "On 11th and

My Beloved Daughter

area BC", was Mel's reply. "I wonder if that could mean the Jacob K. Javits Center. Let's park the car and walk up and find out", said Mel excitedly. As we approached the building we discovered some signs in front, A, B, and C. We checked out the bathrooms, a likely place to find someone who might be homeless. Nobody there. Upstairs there was an exhibit on Chinese culture. Mel and I decided not to let a chance pass. We would even look there as ∀ really liked the oriental look. We quickly looked through and realized that ∀ was not there. Where would we go next?

We decided to go to Times Square Church to ask if anyone had heard of ∀. We talked to a man named John. He had not seen her around, but he encouraged us to continue to show her picture around. Maybe we would get lucky. We told John that we would be back for the evening services at 7:00pm.

Mel then suggested that we go to the Port of Authority to see if we could find anything there. After all, there were many homeless people crowding the hallways there. Maybe we would be successful in finding ∀. We walked around the port for a while until we felt it useless to continue. Then we went to the youth division, just around the corner from the Port of Authority and talked with

Detective Garcia. I explained my daughter's situation to him. He had not seen ∀ in his travels, but took a copy of her photograph in case he came in contact with her. He was not too encouraging. He said the city was very big and easy to get lost in.

Mel and I decided it was time for us to get some lunch. I felt it was also time for me to stop my fast. Mel and I shared a burger at a local restaurant. I even showed ∀'s picture to the waitress. Did she know anything? No, nothing. Our afternoon was taken up with more false starts, but no opportunity to find ∀.

It was now time for Mel and I to make our way to Times Square Church. I was really excited. I felt that this was to be a glorious time. I had always wanted to go to Times Square Church. We entered the church and sat down and waited. Next to Mel sat a young man. It appeared that he was in great distress. Mel asked him what his name was. Tom, it appeared was having a difficult time focusing on the sermon or even the music. He sat rather stone-faced. Mel and I decided to invite him to dinner with us after the service. He agreed, but indicated he had no money for dinner. Mel treated us both at the restaurant. As we talked Tom shared with us that he had not been able to read his Bible; every time he opened it, his mind was blurred. It appeared the Lord had a lot of work to do in Tom. But first He had to get the blinders off Tom. We prayed right then and there for Tom and after our meal bid him a good night.

Then we headed downtown to reach Showworld, where we believed ∀ might have a job. It was early, but we thought we could view what was going on and then maybe wait until she might come outside around 1:00am. From reading ∀'s journals, Mel and I had determined that ∀'s job, if she still had it, started around 5:00pm and ended about 1:00am. As we walked downtown, we approached two teenagers or young adults we believed to be spaced out on drugs. They appeared to be dancing and clapping their hands. Mel said, "Don't get too close to them." So as we skirted around them, we checked them out. Then we recognized their words. They were praising and dancing before the Lord. Mel asked if they had just been at Times Square Church. The young man called Patrick said that they had been there tonight. Immediately Mel and I had the same thought. Maybe these two boys would be willing to go to Showworld Playhouse to ask about ∀ and to see if she was working there tonight. After all, Mel and I did not want to hang around until 1:00am if ∀ was not working tonight. The boys agreed that they would do what they had to if it was for the Lord. At Patrick's suggestion we prayed right there, on the street corner for guidance and safety. Then with the Lord's angels going before us, Patrick, Roy, Mel and I began our trek to 42nd Street. The bouncer told the boys, after eyeing them carefully that ∀ was not working tonight. We walked a while longer and then decided to go to Covenant House. Maybe they had heard of or seen ∀. We talked with some of the people from Covenant House and showed them my daughter's picture. No, they had not seen her. Because it was getting late, we told the boys that we would take them home. So up to Harlem we drove with our Christian tapes blaring in the radio and Patrick and Roy praising the Lord along with Mel and I. As the boys were leaving the car, Patrick shared that the men he was about to step between to go up the stairs to his apartment were crack dealers and they always hung out at that building. Mel and I decided that Patrick and Roy really needed prayer. They were both fairly new Christians of about one-and-a-half to two years and they would need lots of prayer to make it in Harlem. Now it was time for Mel and I to head back to Long Island. Tomorrow was another day, the right day for ∀ to be discovered!

FIVE
NYC Day 2: Looking

Mel and I approached Covenant House to check again today with the morning people about ∀, as had been suggested to us yesterday. We were feeling refreshed and ready for a new day. When we reached Covenant house I asked the attendant if she would be willing to show ∀'s picture to the day people. "I'm quite sure she now has blond hair", I said. "Could she be in there now?" As the attendant left to ask if anyone had seen ∀, I felt a rise in my spirit. After all today was the day we would find ∀. I was quite sure of that. God's timetable had been two days and that timeframe kept recurring to me over and over. Maybe someone had seen her or maybe she was there this morning after having spent the night. The attendant came back and her face told me she had no good news. No one had seen her or knows her. There's only one blonde there and she is tall with long hair. We thanked the attendant and asked her to be on the lookout for my daughter; we gave her Mel's card with her phone number on it. We then introduced ourselves and discovered a new friend in Nancy. She asked about ∀ and her schooling.

"∀ started college at FIT, but failed out last semester. She apparently has gotten herself into some heavy stuff", I told her. Nancy told us she was a student at Hunter College, but on graduation day she would have her bags all packed for her home state of Illinois. She was to graduate with a teaching degree next year and was anxious to get away from New York City. We had hugs all around and wished Nancy a happy 4th of July. Then we started back the way we had come toward 42nd Street.

On our way back to 42nd Street, Mel and I walked by a flower shop. I saw roses and knew I had to purchase one for ∀. But that would be later. We decided to check out the area around Showworld and the Port of Authority. As we approached Showworld we walked by a church. I felt a leading to go into the church to pray and asked Mel about it. She confirmed that was what we were to do, so in we went. We sat down about five pews from the back. There were two or three other people praying in the church. Mel and I immediately started praying. "Lord, I pleaded, this is your church. This may be a catholic church (of which I was unfamiliar), but this is where your people pray so it's your church." I continued to praise the Lord and ask for guidance in seeking my daughter. I had no doubt then that we would find her; after all, I knew where she worked and when she worked. I still had that twinge of doubt about whether she would come with me voluntarily. After Mel and I finished praying we walked outside and headed to Showworld. As we walked, Mel said to me, "Jean, I don't get visions or things like this much, but I want to tell you what I believe the Lord just said to me. As I was praying He asked me if I had the faith that ∀ would be found. I told Him, Yes, Lord, I've never doubted. Then He said to me that He would bring her to us". I got shivers up and down my arms as I always do when I see God's power working. Then Mel continued, "The Lord showed me a tender new shoot like a bean sprout and then it grew like a jack-in-the-beanstalk, quickly and surely. The seed was planted." I thanked Mel for sharing that with me. I knew that she was strengthened by the Holy Spirit's revelation and I was refortified. I believed with all my heart that ∀ would be found today. I also decided that God wanted ∀ saved from these horrifying conditions she was living in. He would help her say yes to accepting help! That had been my fear before. Even though I did not claim that fear, it had pervaded my thinking on occasion and really seemed to be the only doubt about this whole escapade. After all, if ∀ didn't come with me when I found her, what could I do?

Mel and I decided to go into the diner across from Showworld and ask the waitress we had yesterday if she had seen ∀. We sat down in the same seats as the day before and warmly greeted our same waitress. "I'll have a Coke with three ice cubes and Mel, what do you want?" I queried. Mel agreed that a Sprite with lemon sounded good and suggested I show the waitress ∀'s picture. So I took the picture out of my pocket and asked if she had seen my daughter. I told her that ∀ probably had blond hair at this point. The waitress did not recognize ∀, but pointed out two off-duty policemen sitting a few seats away. The waitress suggested we ask them if they had seen my daughter. "Have you seen my daughter? She's probably a blond wearing black clothes now", I entreated. No, they had not seen her, but told us about Officer Gonzales at the Youth Services Bureau. "It might be helpful if you went to see him."

Officer Gonzales was very helpful although he had not seen ∀. He took a copy of her picture in case he ran into her. He told us there were many runaways in New York City. The city was very big and easy to get lost in. Where were we to look next?

I told Mel, "I think we should take a break. I think that we should go to the Empire State Building. I feel the Lord leading it. Actually, Mel, I want to go there; it's my own selfish thought. I do feel the Lord telling us to stop looking. After all, He told you He'd bring ∀ to us. I think that time will be when she goes to work tonight." Mel quickly told me not to limit God. We might even find her at the Empire State Building. Mel agreed that we stop officially looking for ∀ and we started to walk to 34th and 5th Streets. Just a short distance away we saw a McDonald's where ∀ could have purchased coffee. We decided to go into McDonald's as we were both thirsty by then. After I had just made the statement that I felt the Lord wanted us to stop looking, I said "Let's go look and see if ∀ is there". When Mel and I were finishing our drinks after polishing off 6 Mcnuggets, a man approached with two tickets in his hand. He then showed us a card stating he was deaf and could we contribute anything to help his family. Mel and I each gave him some bills and Mel also wrote him a message to go to Times Square Church. She believed he could be healed. The deaf man thanked Mel in his way and we prepared to go out into the hot city streets again.

    We then proceeded straight to the Empire State Building and purchased our entry tickets. It didn't look too busy. Probably everyone was out of the city at the beach today. As we approached the elevators, our countenances fell. There ahead of us were endless people waiting to make the trip to the top. I looked at Mel. Did she want to stay or go. I told Mel again that I thought it was just my own selfish desire to come here. "No, we'll stay", said Mel. The line moved fairly quickly so our decision to stay had been the right one, although we had lots of time until we needed to leave. Our concern was to be back at Showworld by 4:30pm to watch for ∀.

Part way through the wait for the elevator, Mel's face had a look of real concern on it. "I sense something is bothering you", I told her. She said that she was just thinking of her son and we must pray for him. So we started praying, not knowing what in particular to pray for. After a few minutes, Mel shared with me an incident that had happened a while ago when she had hurt his feelings. The Lord had revealed this to Mel as she prayed today. The incident took place at this very same building on a trip Mel and her son had made months before. Praise God, there was a purpose for coming here. "Now you can ask your son's forgiveness", I said encouragingly. We continued up to the observation deck and took some time to look over New York City. What a big place I thought. Where is she? She must be hurting so badly. "Lord", I said.

"I trust you and you promised that you'll bring ∀ to me. I'm standing on that promise."

As we walked from the Empire State Building to Showworld to wait for ∀ we found some steps to sit on. I thought I might have blisters as my feet were so sore and Mel's legs were tired too. We had been walking the hot, dirty streets of New York City for two days now without much rest. As we sat watching people walk by, a young family approached having just made a purchase at McDonald's. Suddenly the bottom fell out of the kid meal carton and hamburger, French fries and soda went toppling out onto the sidewalk. The family stopped, looked and then walked on, obviously frustrated as their little one cried for the lost treat. I said to Mel, "Let's see who picks up the hamburger". It was still wrapped. Mel and I sat and watched as people came and went. Suddenly I saw a man approach whom we had seen sitting in front of Showworld the night before. Last night he had been trying to light his mouth with a cigarette lighter. I thought surely he would take this hamburger. I don't know if he didn't see it or just did not have the desire to eat, but he passed it by. I have always thought of homeless people as hungry people, but it appears that some of these homeless people have more of a need for drugs and alcohol than nourishing food. This thought crossed my mind as I watched what appeared to be two or three "homeless" people walk right on past the burger. We sat for a few minutes longer, checked the time and decided that we needed to start heading back to Showworld. As we walked down the street, Mel pointed out a man who seemed to be following us. It became apparent as we stopped to look at a shop window that we had a professional pickpocket behind us. We went into a store and saw his attention diverted to another young girl who had been walking near us. As if my desire for adventure was not enough, I talked Mel into following him. We kept a decent amount of space between us, but proceeded to follow and observe a professional in action. He was a well-dressed, clean-cut man, probably in his thirties. We continued to walk down the street approaching Showworld, watching our professional work. He had not stolen anything yet, but we thought that it was imminent.

As we got nearer to Showworld, we saw a group of people on a street corner. Mel and I decided that it was a religious group passing out tracts. I was immediately seized with a peace about our search for ∀. What a confirmation from the Lord. How mighty God is. There are many street corners in New York City that religious groups can preach from, but this group had chosen to be right out in front of Showworld. As Mel and I approached, we thought we'd find out if they were from Times Square Church. No, they were another group sharing the Lord's word. We talked a few minutes with them and they started to prepare to go. Our timing was just right. I wonder if they ever knew just what a witness they were to Mel and me that day. I then felt buoyed up for our next forty-five minute wait until we hoped to meet with ∀ as she approached work.

Mel and I decided it would be wise for us to eat something as suppertime was quite near. We went into a little deli one block north of Showworld. We each ordered a sandwich and a drink and sat next to a window relaxing and talking about the day's events. As we talked, Mel pointed out our friendly neighborhood pickpocket working the street corner we sat looking at. We kept watch a few minutes longer as he stood at the corner, crossed the street, stood at the opposite corner, crossed back again to the other side, and stood again looking for an easy mark. Apparently he never found one.

SIX
NYC Day 2: Found

Our best plan, thought Mel and I, was to get to Showworld early so we would be sure to see ∀ as she approached for work that night. But first of all, I had to purchase a rose for my daughter. A single rose had always been a significant gesture in my family. It was a way of saying "great job" after a play. ∀ gave a rose to her piano teacher after her husband's death and a single rose could also mean "I love you". I believed God would have me give ∀ a single rose when I saw her. I went into a store just down the street from Showworld and made my purchase. We were confident that this was the right time to find my daughter. Mel went to case the side door and I took the front door. Because I didn't know how this employer of ∀'s would accept me coming to snatch her away, I was leery of acting like I was looking for someone. One thing I did not want to do was to spook ∀ into running away. I also did not want the obvious Showworld bouncer to get rid of me. I chose to stand one or two car lengths away. It appeared natural just to lean against a parked car, so I did. I sure did not want to appear suspicious. It's hard to be watching for someone and not appear to be watching, especially when I had no idea from which direction she would appear. I didn't know if she would come to the front or the side door. I wasn't really sure what time she would come. About the only thing I was sure of was that she would show up. After all, God had promised that to Mel just this morning while we were in church. As I leaned against the car watching people going in and out of Showworld, I wondered what would bring a person to a place in life where that person would go to a place like Showworld as if it were a grocery store. The faces were so bleak to me. There certainly was no 'peace of God' with these people.

As the hour of 5:00pm approached, I became even more watchful in my unsuspicious way. As I searched the crowd looking for $\forall$ I didn't really know what I'd find. What would she look like now? Was her hair short, long, or all shaved off? Did she have black hair as I remembered her or was she a blonde, brunette, or even multicolored as had become quite the fad? Was she still thin or might she have put on weight? All these questions and I had so much time to think about them while I waited. What had happened to my little girl, my dear, sweet beloved daughter since I saw her last in March? How, and much more important, why had she changed so drastically? As I leaned against the car I had many thoughts going through my mind. I knew the Lord would bring ∀ to us as He had promised. As I waited, Mel came around the corner with her face lit up. She explained that she had been talking to the back door bouncer and thought she might have an in there to find out about ∀. Off she went back around the corner to her waiting assignment. More time went by and I began to have doubtful feelings creep in. I started thinking, what if ∀ didn't show up? What if we didn't find her? Where could she be; it was already past 5:00pm, the time Mel and I thought she had to be to work according to her journal. Where was she? My doubt started to produce a real fear unlike anything I had felt since I had first arrived in New York City to search for my daughter. The fear started to grip me, but I took control. I almost literally shouted, "You promised me God. I'm going to hold you to your promise. I expect to see her soon." (2Timothy 1:7). As the fear subsided I became confident again that we would find her. I didn't know when, and by this point, I didn't even really know where. I just felt God's peace come over me. I knew He had the whole situation under control. As I kept looking over the crowds, watching to see from which direction she would come, I felt the peace. I knew I would see my daughter today.

As I continued to watch the crowd, ∀ appeared crossing to my side of the street. She went into the corner store just down the street, the very same store that I had purchased her rose in not more than an hour before. I kept my eyes riveted on the door as I skirted around people to get to the door of the store. The Lord's words, "MY BELOVED DAUGHTER" kept going through my mind in a singsong fashion, as it had been doing all day long. I knew that I must tell her that she was His Beloved Daughter when I first spoke to her. As I opened the door she was standing at the checkout register, the clerk ringing up her juice and magazine. I put my arm on her shoulder and she turned around to face me. As we hugged each other, I gave her the rose and said to her, "∀, the Lord wants me to tell you that you are His Beloved Daughter". She asked what I was doing there. I told her I had come down to see her. I wasn't yet sure what her needs were or even if she wanted me there, but I asked about her going to work. She said she had twenty minutes, as she was early. It seems she did not have to be to work until 5:30pm. I said to ∀, "Let's walk". We walked back past the main entrance to Showworld and then turned the corner toward the side entrance. As we approached the side entrance Mel was nowhere in sight. Where did she go? Maybe inside? I told ∀ to wait one minute and walked up to the open side door. There was Mel talking to someone. I called her, "I have ∀; come on". Mel came out the door and I reintroduced her to ∀. After all, my daughter and Mel had not seen each other since ∀ was five years old. I doubted ∀ even remembered Mel. We talked and briefly caught up as we walked back to the car, which was in a parking garage a short distance away. I pleaded with ∀, "I cannot let you go back in there. You must come with us so I can get you help. I can get you on a plane to a hospital tonight. Please come with me ∀. I can't go home without you." As we talked Mel put her arms around ∀ from behind just to buoy her up. ∀ seemed so fragile. It seemed that Mel was holding on to her so she would not slip away. Would she go with us? After many questions, my daughter decided to go with us. It seems she had signed herself up to go to Beth Israel Hospital for a detox program this coming Monday. I guess she knew how much she needed help. We got into the car and headed back to Showworld for ∀ to pick up her things. As I walked with ∀ through the doors of this pornographic playhouse, my heart sank. I felt so sad for these people from the very depths of my heart. The feeling was not just for ∀ and her co-workers, but for the people who frequented a place like this. Their lives must have been so empty. Thank God I had Jesus in my heart. No matter how low I got, I still could do better than this with God's help.

After ∀ got her things and talked with her boss we were back at the car. This time we were leaving New York City with a victory. The battle was surely not over, hardly even begun, but there was a victory already and I felt the victory march beginning. We headed out of the city and back to Long Island. Our next quest was to find a store open as ∀ needed some personal items before she could board the airplane to get help. However, today was the 4th of July and it was already well past 5pm. All stores seemed to be closed. We finally found a little drug store that was open and went in to make our purchases. Then we wound our way back to Mel's house.

When we got there no one else was home so we had some time to rest and clean up. When ∀ was in the shower Mel called ∀'s father and asked him to call back in a short while to talk to his daughter. I encouraged him to let her know how much he loved her, although I wasn't even sure if he did at this point. My next call was to Rapha to firm up our evening reservations to a Rapha hospital. By the time ∀ got finished showering and had received the phone call from her dad and sorted and packed her things to go, Rapha had firmed up the hospital reservations in Houston, Texas. I felt really good about Houston because that was the city that popped into my mind when I was told the five or six possible cities earlier in the week. It had all depended on when we found her and what room was available in each city. We still had a problem though. The flight was not leaving until 6:50am. There were absolutely no flights out of New York tonight, as I had been assured. When Mel and I found this out we looked at each other and laughed uproariously. God sure had a sense of humor. We now had a big problem! We knew that I could not bring ∀ on a flight for Houston the next morning when she would already be in the midst of withdrawals. The only thing we could do was go back into New York City so she could get her drugs!

    Let me share something about myself with you readers. I grew up in a very old fashioned way. I never smoked a cigarette or did any kind of drugs. I wasn't even keen on taking an aspirin, maybe two or three times a year I'd take one aspirin for a headache. My husband had smoked cigarettes, but had given them up just before we met. I had no friends that were drug addicts, so I was in new territory, brand new territory.

∀ was beginning to feel some weariness and the ever present fear of withdrawals was beginning to eat at her every second of the passing time. "Let's get going. Let's hope the traffic is light", said Mel. Because it was the 4th of July we headed for the Cross Island Expressway toward New York City. Now the task began, as we seemed to be creeping along. "Where is it we need to be going ∀? What's the quickest and best way to get there? Do you want me to carry your drug things for you?" I asked. "No", said ∀. "This is my problem. I own it. If we get stopped I certainly don't want you carrying anything." We went a little further along rather slowly and then our progress picked up. We approached Alphabet City. As we turned down the next street ∀ pointed out the café where Mel was to wait for us as we went to purchase the heroin. As I got out of the car I grabbed ∀'s rose. I was sure God was with us, but maybe the rose would be a sign for ∀ if we had problems. We started down the street at a fast pace, ∀ and I chatting a bit as we walked. There was no fear in me even though it was now past 9:00pm and we were in Alphabet City. I knew that God had blessed this trip into New York City from the very beginning and if this was what had to be done then I knew I had God's approval. I could not put ∀ on an airplane for three hours with heroin withdrawals.

She would never be able to sign herself into the Rapha unit at the Texas hospital. She had to be somewhat calm when we reached Houston.

As we walked down the street where the drugs were to be purchased we noticed firecrackers were going off near the house where we needed to go. I told ∀ not to worry everything would be fine. "Stay close", said ∀ as we approached the apartment building where many people were milling around. Up the steps went ∀ with me close behind. "Hi, Steve. This is my mom". The man known as Steve let ∀ and I pass. We walked down a hallway to a man standing on the stairs. "This is my mom. How's fifty dollars?", said ∀. He gave her four tiny bags in exchange for the fifty dollars supplied by me, her mother. As we walked back down the street all sorts of things were going through my head like I wonder what ∀'s supplier thought of her mother going to buy her drugs. I felt so ashamed and inadequate. However, this man Steve didn't seem to think twice about it. Maybe this was normal, a family thing where parents and children purchase their drugs together. What a dreadful thought.

We now headed to the café where we were to meet Mel. ∀ would go to the bathroom and I would sit with Mel waiting for ∀ to come out. Mel had ordered an avocado salad along with a beer. I ordered a Coke, no ice. Mel and I waited a while for ∀ to come out of the bathroom. When ∀ finally did come out, she quickly found her way to our table. She sat there for a minute as I asked her if everything was OK in my best secret voice. She quietly told me she had broken her needle and would need to purchase another set of "the works". This meant we would have to go back to the street where we had just purchased the drugs. Here she would find another needle for sale. I think the going rate was four dollars. My heart raced again, as we headed back to the street where I would have to now purchase a needle for my daughter to shoot up her heroin. After ∀ got the second needle we went back to the café and met Mel again. This time, after sitting just a few minutes, ∀ reappeared from the bathroom and we left the café. It was now after 10:00pm and we still had more to do before the airplane took off at 6:50am.

Now it was ∀'s desire to visit a homeless friend of hers in Thompson Square. His name was Teddy, a black man who had befriended ∀. He was a drug addict too ∀ explained, but he was intelligent. She could converse with him unlike so many other addicts who had burnt themselves out. He was different she explained. As we approached Thompson Square with all the bodies lying around, some in sleeping bags, others with just what was on their backs laying on park benches, I felt an overwhelming sense of despair. I'm sure many of these people had that same feeling, but for different reasons than I had. I also felt a sense of peace knowing ∀ was being brought out of that scene, through the grace of God. We found Teddy on his bench and ∀ introduced him to me. We talked for a while and ∀ then shared that she was headed to a hospital for recovery. We said our goodbyes and I felt a strong urge to pray fervently for Teddy. In fact, this feeling was so strong that I put Teddy on my church prayer list for quite some time. I believed that God wanted to bless Teddy, in a way I couldn't even imagine.

Now we had one more thing to do before morning. ∀ had some clothes stored at a friend's apartment in Staten Island. We headed for the Staten Island Ferry hoping to get on the 11:00pm ride. We had intended to pick up ∀'s clothes and get back on the ferry for the return trip at 12:00 midnight. As we waited I kept a keen eye out for anyone who was suspicious looking. ∀ was now carrying illegal drugs and paraphernalia. Were there police or undercover cops around? The area was very busy. I also did not want anyone to bump into any of us and be off with anything important. ∀ was beginning to tire. As we sat and waited for the ferry Mel and I were alert for anything out of the ordinary while ∀ tried to relax. Finally, the ferry approached. As we boarded the ferry we decided to find a comfortable place where we were not too conspicuous. We sat outside. There was just enough breeze for me to be cool, but not uncomfortable. On the other hand, ∀ was very cold. She snuggled against Mel's shoulder and actually dozed a bit.

When the ferry landed we quickly departed and walked up the street toward the apartment where we would find ∀'s things. We walked silently by many houses talking quietly about the appearance of the streets and other things. Finally, we reached the apartment. ∀ told us to be very quiet so we would not disturb anyone. We located the door and went silently in. What a mess! Clothes were strewn all over the place, the bed had no sheets, and I just felt dirt all over in this apartment. ∀ sorted through clothes, taking some, leaving others. We then prepared for our return trip to the ferry. We had a fifteen-minute walk back to the ferry terminal and a couple of big bags to tote. But we could do it. As I looked at my watch I realized the time was now 11:45pm. This would be a close call. "Let's hurry. We must get back in time", I said. "Otherwise we will have to pay another ten dollars for Mel's car in the ferry parking lot." We walked as fast as we could with ∀'s bags of clothes, but I had the sinking feeling we would miss the ferry. Sure enough, we got back to the terminal just in time to see the ferry pull away from the dock. That meant another half hour wait for the next and last ferry back to Manhattan.

The ride back was a peaceful one. We had taken care of all the business that was necessary before we left New York City for Houston. Now we had just a few short hours before we drove to LaGuardia for our flight. ∀ told us we needed to look for a place to stop so she could use the last of her heroin. She had saved a dose for this morning so she would be doped up for the flight to Houston. ∀ had never flown before and that was worrying her. She was also concerned because I was not able to tell her that she would be put on methadone as the drug to help detox her. In fact, Rapha had assured me that they did not just substitute one drug for another, but detoxification would be the safest and surest way without any unnecessary drugs. Mel decided that we needed gas and the ladies room of a gas station would be the safest place for ∀ to shoot up. We drove for a short while and stopped at the next gas station. ∀ told us she'd be a few minutes and we made it a point to act natural. How could I as a parent act natural when my little girl was a few feet away shooting up heroin? I was so afraid of the illegal aspect of the drugs especially with me allowing this to take place. I did understand the leading and protection of the Holy Spirit in this case though and was able to relax a bit. After we filled Mel's gas tank and stood waiting a few minutes for ∀ we were aware of the possibility of a question entering the attendant's mind. Why was this girl taking so long? I casually said to Mel within hearing of the attendant, "I hope ∀ is not feeling sick again like she was earlier this evening". Finally ∀ came out and we all piled into the car. Now we had to dispose of the needle. Where could we throw it that it would not be a problem? We did not want anyone to find it or get hurt on it. After all, I had seen many people going through trash receptacles while I was here in New York City. We drove around a bit and discovered a police station. We decided that we needed to drive a bit longer, further from the police station. We finally felt comfortable stopping at a garbage can and ∀ quickly disposed of the syringe she had broken in half. Now everything was taken care of so we could board the airplane and ∀ could begin her life again. We had gotten her things out of her locker at Showworld, we had purchased some things for her to take to the hospital in Houston, we had cleaned her clothes out of her friend's apartment, we had visited Teddy, and finally ∀ had shot up what I prayed would be the very last dose of heroin.

It was now about 5:00am. Mel and I had been up for at least twenty-four hours now. It was time to head to the airport where, in less than two hours ∀ and I would be on an airplane to Houston. This would be my first plane ride on a commercial jet. I was excited, but I was also concerned for ∀. I did not want to let her out of my sight. The Lord had led me to New York City to find ∀, and I was thankful for that gift, but we were only half way there. ∀ still had to sign herself in to the hospital. She could easily run when we got off the airplane if she was scared enough. Or she could run now while we were still in New York City. I must keep watching!

SEVEN

Day 3: Flight To Houston

When we reached LaGuardia Airport it was approaching 6:10am. We gave hugs and love to Mel after we unloaded our bags from her trunk. I felt that this closed a chapter in my life. I do not even know how to explain the closeness I felt toward Mel in just these last three days. I guess when a friend goes into the pit of Hell for you and provides for you in numerous ways like meals, ferry rides and parking, driving you all around while you look for your daughter, and waiting while you go buy drugs...this is the ultimate in being Christ-like as Jesus calls us Christians to be. Mel, I can never thank you enough for what you have given my daughter!

The Continental Airline desk was just opening up, the lights were turned on and the door unlocked. ∀ and I made our way into the terminal to get our tickets. Then we had enough time to get a light breakfast in the little café next to our waiting area. ∀ went through the line first so I could watch the bags. Her corn muffin looked so good that I decided to try a muffin, a cup of tea and a juice. After we ate I suggested to ∀ that there might be a little shop here at the airport that would have some makeup she was looking for and had not been able to find yesterday. ∀ asked me to go look, but repeated again the exact makeup that she needed. The little shop had some cosmetics but not the kind ∀ needed. I went back empty handed. "Sorry, ∀. This store did not carry it and the other airport pharmacy does not open until 7:00am. We'll be on the plane by then". Off to the bathroom I went to wash my face, clean my teeth and take care of other necessities. Then it was time to head to the boarding gate.

We boarded the plane, stowed our bags and settled into our seats. ∀ was unsettled as she had never flown in an airplane. I had flown just once in my life when I was about eleven or twelve years old. I flew in a 4-seater seaplane with my dad and brother. My enthusiasm for flying was certainly not very encouraging to ∀ and as much as I wanted to share my excitement, I could see it was not helpful to ∀. So I tried to keep quiet. Do you know what it is like to contain a small child's wonder at the zoo? I felt that same excitement about my upcoming airplane ride and containing it was difficult. Once we were airborne, ∀ seemed to be relieved. I felt a lifting of my spirits, something akin to ecstasy, as the airplane lifted off the ground. I thought too bad ∀ couldn't feel this, but

My Beloved Daughter

I knew she was too afraid of the heroin withdrawals that she had yet to go through. She was ticking off those hours until the withdrawal symptoms began. She had shot up her last two bags of heroin around 5:00am and time was ticking by. We were scheduled to arrive in Houston at 9:46am CT, which is 10:46 EST, almost six hours after her last dose of heroin. How would she do?

After we had climbed to our travel height the airplane leveled off and our stewardess came around with juice and breakfast: cereal, a banana, milk and a muffin. "∀, here's your banana." ∀ had wanted a banana last night, but the store we went to had all kinds of fruit and no bananas. In a short while, ∀ got up and headed toward the bathroom. After about ten minutes passed I realized that this could mean only one thing. She must not be feeling well. So much for breakfast and her banana.

It was now descent time. What a different feeling coming down in an airplane was than taking off. It was a fairly smooth ride down although we had a couple of quick drops, which left our stomachs up in the air. When we finally did land it started raining. We were to meet a limo driver who would be wearing a big red Rapha button. As we left the airplane, Gordon, our driver was easy to spot. I introduced myself and ∀ to him and we proceeded to the escalators which took us down to the baggage area. I told Gordon that our luggage was what we were carrying, so we went back up the escalator to the parking area. Gordon tried hard to make us feel comfortable and welcome. I enjoyed his hospitality, but ∀ was not nearly as receptive. ∀ asked if we could stop and get makeup on the way to the hospital. Gordon said he knew of a drugstore on the way. So off we went in what was now a downpour. The rain came so fast and so abundantly that there were actually rivers of water running down the sides of the road. Gordon told us he had just washed his limousine that morning. I laughed. I wasn't surprised.

After getting the makeup and a little further drive, Gordon pulled into the Sharpstown General Hospital parking area. He helped us with our luggage and then took his leave of us. ∀ and I sat in admissions waiting to be processed. I kept thanking the Lord that He was continuing to be faithful. Then it was my daughter's turn for admission. She gave her name. When the receptionist asked for her address ∀ blurted out, "I'm homeless". I quickly told the receptionist she could put my address down. After lots of papers were signed, ∀ reading each one carefully as I had always taught my children to do, we were then escorted upstairs to the Rapha unit, the top floor of this hospital. ∀ was taken to a room to be checked in. I was introduced to Eric Scolese, the Rapha administrator at Sharpstown Hospital. Eric invited me into an office to talk. It seems that there might be some concern about her insurance. ∀'s insurance would only cover five days in the hospital for detoxification and then no inpatient rehabilitation. She could have sixty days for outpatient rehabilitation. I listened thoroughly to Eric and then calmly stated, "I didn't bring my daughter all the way from New York City after what we've been through to find out she only has five days. That is not enough. I'm trusting the Lord to find a way for the thirty days." Boy, one more notch in my faithbelt! Right then and there I spoke to the Lord Jesus Christ. "God, I know that you can work out whatever has to be. I believe that you didn't bring ∀ all the way here just to have her kicked out in five days because of her insurance." Again I said to the Lord, "This is yours to deal with. I can't. Thank you, Lord." I told Eric to do what he had to do and I'd be trusting the Lord to work it out. I was then shown to ∀'s room. I made sure she was as comfortable as she could be considering the circumstances and then prepared to go to the hotel to check in.

    I thanked the cab driver and approached the front

desk to get signed in. It seems everything was quickly done and I got into my room between four and five o'clock in the afternoon. I had not slept since Tuesday night and then for only about six hours. It was now Thursday, late afternoon and although I had not slept for thirty-six hours, I was prepared to stay awake longer if need be to help my daughter. God had shown me that with His power I could do anything for my daughter that He required of me. I had a great view out the window. I was on the fourth floor overlooking the pool, which looked like a tropical garden. I was staying at the Tides II Motel at 6700 S. Main Street in Houston. This was a rather strange coincidence when I stopped to think that the Sharpstown Hospital was located on 6700 Bellaire. I knew I was in the right hotel. My room had two double beds and a small living area at one length of the room with a table, chair and a full picture window. I opened the curtains and made a couple of phone calls. Then it was time to sleep. Just before I fell asleep, I felt the Lord nudging me to write this story. I slept until around 6:00am the next morning.

EIGHT
∀'s Path to Addiction

New York City in 1989 was so far away from what I was used to as a small town girl growing up in upstate NY that I couldn't imagine all the things that must go on 'down there'. However, as ∀ told me how she first became addicted and took her first jump into the abyss of drugs, my heart was crying out for her and for others who may begin the drug addiction in this very same way. Thus began the saga of Teen ∀'s year of destruction of her beautiful body and wonderful mind.

∀ told me she had a "brief" introduction to LSD, Ecstasy, and Cocaine while in her first year at FIT College. I had no idea that she had tried these drugs. Then she said she had decided to snort 'coke' during her midterms when a friend offered it to her. She said it felt like being in heaven. She then asked her friend what it was, as she did not think it was Cocaine. He told her it was Heroin. She was angry with him, as she had vowed never to do Heroin. She felt it was an end-of-the-line kind of drug and wanted nothing to do with it. However, about a month later she did try it one more time when she went with a friend to Alphabet city for the friend to purchase some drugs. Her 'thank-you' gift was a small packet of drugs – yes, that's right Heroin. Well, one more time wouldn't matter. After that experience, ∀ thought she had the flu as she was having cold chills and sweats, sneezing and nausea. The 'flu' turned into a full fledged addiction to Heroin. Within four more months, ∀ felt that her heaven had brought her into hell, as she told me.

NINE
Houston - the Days After

When I awoke after my first night of sleep in two days, I felt refreshed and alert. I went down to the hotel dining room and ordered Eggs Benedict for breakfast. I was really looking forward to this treat as I had served them many times at my waitress job and I rarely found them on breakfast menus when I went out to eat. But, my waiter came back and told me he had no sauce for the eggs. I ordered eggs over light, hash browns, bacon and juice. I needed to be fortified today to do the things that needed to be done. I must get ∀ some sneakers and socks. I decided to go look for some writing materials as I needed to get all the information I could down on note cards so I could be accurate in writing this story. It is important to me to be accurate. I was really excited to start writing this story. God kept prompting me with ideas. After breakfast I showered and got my tote bag and purse.

I started out the front door. Which way should I go? I guess I'll go to the right. There was a bank in that direction, I thought and definitely a Burger King for lunch. I had plenty of leg strength and I knew I could walk a great distance if I had to. After all, I had just walked New York City for two days. I walked down the street looking for a shoe store and a drug store in which to purchase writing materials. I must have walked about two miles up one street looking for stores to suit my needs but nothing was available. It was approaching lunchtime and I decided to stop into Burger King to get a drink and something quick to eat. I could visit ∀ at 2:00pm so I needed to have my shopping finished by then. After lunch I headed back to the hotel and was told that just down the street there was an Eckhard drugstore. Here I found my paper, note cards and notebook. After checking out I went back to the hotel to call a taxi for my trip back to Sharpstown General Hospital to see ∀.

As I got into the taxi and gave my instructions I discovered a very friendly driver by the name of Jesse. As we talked and I told him just a little about my circumstances, I discovered that he was a Christian man. As I told Jesse about my desire to write ∀'s story he shared with me that his wife had once sent in a story to Guideposts, a small Christian magazine. Apparently it was not accepted for publication but I nevertheless felt a bond with this man. With all the taxi drivers in Houston how had I been able to get a Christian man to drive me to the hospital? God was surely at work again. This seemed to be another confirmation to start a book. Jesse also explained that busses ran the very same route from the hospital to my hotel so I should have no problem in the future getting where I needed to go at a less expensive rate. This was a straight route although probably five miles or more. I couldn't get lost.

When I got to the hospital to visit ∀ that day I didn't quite know what to expect. Had my daughter been faring ok with withdrawals? The nurse told me ∀ had been going through withdrawals for quite a while complaining of stomach cramps and such. In fact when I arrived I found ∀ rubbing a pendant and ring asking for relief from her cramps and imagined seizures. The nurse and I looked at each other and the nurse immediately removed the pendant and ring. "These will be kept in our safe for you until you are ready to go home", said the nurse. I agreed.

After I had been visiting ∀ for about three hours, I decided to try out the bus thing. I have never ridden a bus much and I wasn't real sure about what to do. How much was the bus fare? Did I have to have exact change or would the bus driver be able to give me change? Did I have to pull a cord to stop the bus? I crossed the street and approached the bus waiting area. Boy was the day hot! It sure was July and I was not used to all this humidity. I could feel the water just running down the middle of my back. I don't think I ever sweat that much just standing still before. I courageously conquered the bus ride and arrived back at my room saturated in sweat.

When I talked to Mel on the phone that night, she told me she would be arriving in Houston tomorrow to see ∀. I was pleased that Mel had felt led to come see ∀. This was quite an expense for a single working woman although see was able to get a great rate to come. When we arrived at the hospital ∀ was surprised and pleased to see Mel and the afternoon went so quickly.

When it was time to leave the hospital, Mel and I decided to go to a Mexican restaurant Mel had seen on her drive to the hospital. We ate quite a meal, Mexican all the way. That night Mel and I took a walk around the area of the motel. Rice University was just a short walk away and we were excited because there was to be a summit conference at Rice University, to begin this very weekend. President Bush would be here along with a delegation from Russia. We wondered what type of security we would find. We wondered if we would be stopped by anyone asking why we were walking around the university after midnight. It

MY BELOVED DAUGHTER

was so warm and beautiful at this time of night. And Mel and I had so much to talk about. We relived some of the time in New York City. We walked past trees and bushes, garden areas and flower spots. Mel was there for me again I marveled, just as she had been this past week when I really needed her. God had surely placed her back in my life for a purpose. That purpose was unfolding before my very eyes. As we walked and talked I felt a sense of peace flood into my heart. I felt so thankful that my daughter, God's Beloved Daughter, was still alive. If she were in New York City right now, she'd be just getting out of work probably heading to a place to shoot up more drugs. God is so good; He had saved my daughter's life, using Mel and me as we obediently followed His instructions.

The next day was Sunday and time for Mel to go home. I was so thankful that she was able to come to Houston to see ∀. It seemed that this chapter of our lives had to continue together just a while longer. It was hard to say goodbye, but I would be flying back to Long Island soon and then driving back to Glens Falls to wait for ∀'s recovery.

The Rapha unit at Sharpstown General Hospital holds a service on Sunday mornings. I went with ∀ although I thought she would rather sit this one out, but she had no choice. It was a requirement for all the patients to be at services. ∀ sat across the room from me and I watched her as the service progressed. She really wanted to be out of that room, but I was thankful for God's word. I do not recall much about that service except that one of the songs we sang was Because He Lives. I felt the presence of the Lord very clearly then and knew that I had done the right thing in bringing my daughter here. ∀ will tell you differently! The scripture reading that Sunday was from Micah 2. The message was clear. I sure hoped ∀ was in for some loving from our Heavenly Father. She needed to be healed from all the turmoil in her life. Why could I see that so clearly and to ∀ it was not at all visible?

Day 7, Monday, July 9 was to be a very busy day. I awoke early and decided it was time to call ∀'s insurance to find out what options we had for her stay at Sharpstown General Hospital. I discovered that she was covered for only five days of treatment as an inpatient and for two weeks as an outpatient. There was no way that we could even consider outpatient status as we had no funding to stay in Texas. ∀ could not stay alone; I would have to stay with her and where could we afford to stay? I pondered this situation knowing that the Lord was in control. There was one bit of encouragement as I spoke with one of the youth workers back at my home church. The youth had just sponsored a salad bar to raise money for a trip to a youth conference the next year and they wanted the money to go to ∀. They had made one-hundred sixty dollars. Super!

I had packed the night before so all that remained of my preparations to get to the airplane for my trip home was to shower and get to the bus stop for the shuttle to the airport. The shuttle was to arrive at 9:30am, which would get me to the airport a good hour ahead of time. As I waited at the bus stop and continued to wait and wait I became a little more unsettled. This was just the start of my trip home. After I got on the plane at 11:20am and reached New York City, I would then have a four-hour drive to my own home. I was not looking forward to this long day, but the thought of missing my plane was even more disheartening. What could I do? It occurred to me that the Lord knew exactly what needed to be done to get me to the plane on time. Maybe I should pray! Immediately the shuttle bus came. Pat, the driver, indicated that all the busses were running late because of the summit and the extreme heavy traffic. Pat had a knee injury and had a son with a broken ankle. I told her I would pray for them both. With that we had a safe journey to the airport and I arrived in time for my flight. As the airplane approached New York City we seemed to be in the midst of heavy rain. It appeared that there would be a delay in landing. When we finally landed it did not take long for me to call Mel and have her reach me. Then back to Mel's home and load my bags into the car and head north out of the city. The four hours went rather smoothly. Even though I was tired, I made the trip home uneventfully. Thank you, Lord.

Our Albany area had been in the midst of preparations for a Billy Graham Crusade since early winter. As God would have it, I was able to attend the crusade on Saturday. What a blessing to see all these people hungry for Jesus Christ. I wished that ∀ had not fallen so far behind in her walk with the Lord. I realized that she had a difficult road ahead of her and I very much wished she could see what I was looking at here at the crusade. Hundreds, maybe a thousand or more, people coming forward at the invitation of Billy Graham. How I wished ∀ was in the midst of that group.

Sunday at church I asked my pastor if I could have a few minutes of time in the pulpit to share with the congregation about my trip to New York City and also to ask for help. I really felt that with me working full time I would need some people to minister to ∀ when I was gone all day long, once she returned home. I talked with the congregation sharing a little of my trip to New York City, about God's timing, humor and faithfulness. I told about Mel's vision in the church that we had chosen to pray in. I told about how God had shared the words I was to use when I saw my daughter and that I was to buy her a rose. I shared a picture that God had given me of a triangle with the words FAITH, FAITHFULNESS, and OBEDIENCE at each one of the points and in the center tying it all together was PRAYER. I also needed a place to store some of ∀'s things that I felt were important to her, but also a hindrance to her at this point. Friends of mine were willing to store the two plastic bags in their garage. Thank you, Lord for good friends, friends in the Lord.

After church it was time for me to head back to the airport in New York City to return to Houston. ∀ was to be released Monday morning and I would be there to pick her up and bring her home to Glens Falls. My plan was to go to Long Island again and Mel would take me to the airport. I could again leave my car with the family where Mel lived.

When we got to the airport it appeared that my plane was running late according to the departure schedule. I would not be able to make my connection at

Raleigh-Durham so I was scheduled on a Continental flight, first class, in fact. The flight went straight through to Houston with no connecting flight. I found the time restful and experienced an interesting look into the upper class. I was served warm, just baked cookies after being offered a warm towelette to wipe my hands on. With all of this luxury, I still did not arrive until close to 11:00pm. I rented a car, the money for that being provided by people in my church, and then I headed for my hotel. Tomorrow was to be another long day and I needed some rest. It would be good to see my daughter tomorrow and see how much improvement there would be. I wished we could have worked out her hospital stay for at least a month, but twelve days was better than no days.

I arrived at Sharpstown General Hospital and ∀ was ready to go. After saying her goodbyes and introducing me to her friend Randy, we were off to the airport. She seemed a little nervous, but I thought the airplane flight was again an area of concern for her. We only had two bags for ∀ and one for me plus my purse. When we got to the airport we were able to get close to the gate to be able to get on the plane as soon as we were allowed. This flight had a stopover at Raleigh-Durham, but it was only a short layover, which I was glad for. By now, with my daughter in tow, I was anxious to get back to Long Island and head home. During the flight ∀ was able to sleep which I thought was a good thing. Little did I realize that she had kept a sleeping pill just for this airplane flight home.

By the time we landed at Raleigh-Durham, I was concerned that ∀ was not able to get moving quickly. As a matter of fact, she was resting heavily on my arm as we exited the plane. As I perused the flight board, it appeared our next flight was boarding in twenty minutes all the way at the other end of the airport. First we needed to stop at the restroom; then I could think about how to get us there on time. My arms were loaded down with three heavy bags and a purse. As if that was not enough, I was supporting my daughter as she walked along. Finally, I saw a cart approaching and I asked if we could hop on to make our flight in time. Yes, the driver said. We arrived at the gate about five minutes before they closed the gate. I had just enough time to run get my daughter some gum she requested and then we boarded the plane.

The flight to New York was uneventful. ∀ appeared to get more refreshed the closer we got to New York City. Mel met us at the airport and took us out to dinner before we went to her house and retrieved my car. After we said our goodbyes, ∀ and I headed home to the house she grew up in, the house I hoped she would find peace in as she continued to heal emotionally.

TEN
The Years After

This chapter is meant for an encouraging interpretation of the years of struggle that go into growing up from a child into a teenager and then into a young adult. My daughter is now in her forties and a wonderful caring adult. Although ∀ will tell you she still has an addiction, my daughter has not used illegal drugs for many years. In fact, over ten years ago she gave up cigarettes also, having smoked them since she was a late teen. She is careful what she puts into her body now and has helped many people along the way with their addictions. I am sorry that she had to undergo such a hard time growing up from teen to adult, but I am also thankful to God for how he protected her many times and how he brought me to New York City when I needed to be there for my daughter.

∀ has since repaired her relationship with her father, after a ten-year struggle with him. They now are able to talk and spend quality time together. I am thankful for that as I know how valuable a dad's opinion of his "little girl" can be to a young woman. In this entire situation,

I am thankful God gave me unconditional love for my daughter. I could not have loved her unconditionally as I approached Showworld that fateful July day if God had not given me His eyes to see her with.

Since this experience I have been active in doing jail ministry weekly at two local jails. Understanding what my daughter went through and how addicting drugs are has given me a real heart to minister to the men and women I see each week in the jails. Every week I go into the jails, God gives me His heart to love the women and His eyes to see them with. I tell them that I do not see them in their stripes (jailclothes), but beautiful as God sees them. We do a Bible study and in this process if I can help even just one person, I am thankful for I know my God is an AWESOME GOD. I have seen many people changed as they come to know the love Jesus has for them, even as jail inmates. Many inmates have shared with me that they believe God is working in their lives because they are now off the street and in a place where God can use their incarceration time for their spiritual growth. Beyond a doubt, living in this world is far better with Jesus walking beside you. As He shows you what needs to be done for "the least of these", I pray you might respond to all of God's children as if they were your own. Nothing can be more exhilarating than knowing you have made a difference in someone's life. But, it is not about the feeling of exhilarating, it is about God's command to go to the "least of these" and make a difference (Matt25:40).

About the Author

Jean Parthat trusted in God to help her daughter escape the abyss of addiction, and she hopes My Beloved Daughter can help other parents of teens with addiction pray and better understand the power of God in horrendous situations where there seems to be no way out.

Printed in the United States
By Bookmasters